for R...

Happy ...y!

GREAT APES

*A Shrewdness of Poetic Imitations
and Other Follies*

Ken Moffat & James Soderholm

Kind regards, Prof. Soderholm Ken Moffat

LANGTON PRESS

First published 2015 by
Langton Press
Langton Lane, Nackington Road,
Canterbury, Kent, CT4 7AS
United Kingdom
www.langtonpress.co.uk

British Library Cataloguing-in-Publication Data
A CIP catalogue record for this book is available from the British Library

ISBN 978-0-9932-1631-2 (paperback)

Langton Press Logo design by Michael Thundow

Cover illustration and design by Joey Howe
Graphic Design by Liz Jones

Printed and bound in Great Britain by
Parkers Design and Print, Canterbury, Kent

Poetry is what we do to break bread with the dead.

Seamus Heaney

For Molly Moffat
who gave me words, words, words...

And for Donna Soderholm
who tried to keep the heart light

Contents

Thanksgiving

We would first like to thank Christina Moss for looking over the manuscript at a relatively early stage and offering invaluable suggestions as well as generally giving the thumbs up to the project and, sensibly, encouraging the *Legends* section of the book. Her wisdom, depth of knowledge and understanding of English Literature both re-assured and inspired us.

Professor Kevin Cole of the University of Sioux Falls, South Dakota, a fellow poet, gave tremendous support and encouragement to the work and we offer our gratitude.

Highest praise for Janeen Barker, without whom this book would not have reached the upper limbs.

A big thanks to all the staff at The Goods Shed, Canterbury, where much of this book was re-drafted, re-fashioned and, in some cases, written. Paulina, in particular, kept us refreshed as we broke bread with the dead.

Thanks to colleague and artist, Andy Howe, who advised on the artwork and to artist, Joey Howe, and graphic designer, Liz Jones, for the cover illustration and design.

To the wonderful team at Parkers Design and Print, especially to Klaudyna for her patience and meticulous labours.

And thanks for support and promotion from Dr Martin Latham at Waterstones, Canterbury, where this book was launched on the 26th November, 2015: Thanksgiving Day.

And finally, thanks to Carol Ann Duffy whose visit to the Langton in 2014 firmly set the ape ball rolling.

Preface

Poetic imitation of one's masters and the ludic art of pastiche have evolved a few minor achievements. We note, in particular, Isaac Hawkins Browne's parody of Swift and Pope, *A Pipe of Tobacco* (1736) and Rudyard Kipling's *The Muse Among the Motors* (1900-1930). Our slender volume contributes to this sub-genre of poetry. We wanted greatly to ape our poetic predecessors in a way that intoxicates, rather than sobers, readers of fairly sincere forms of flattery. Our intention has been to continue this history of imitation in order, occasionally, to throw new light on old masters; and, after all, most editions of *The Collected Keats* begin with his 'Imitation of Spenser'.

On a technical note, many of these poems are genuinely the work of two minds, collaborations with stanzas written in turn and bandied back and forth, whilst others are largely solo contributions subjected to dual, and sometimes duel, tweaking afterwards. We hope the stitching doesn't show. Genuine literary collaboration is rare and we have had to put our egos in a box to achieve this.

Where we have used anachronisms, we make little apology. Chaucer would have had an ipadde, given half the chance, and Marvell backed so many dodgy politicians in his time, why not Tony Blair? On occasion we have not just resorted to parody, but produced poems we wish our heroes and heroines would have written, had they only world enough and time.

Whilst having a little gentle fun at the expense of the greats of the past and the present, and sometimes using them as a platform to explore postures new, we promise that the iconoclast's hammer has been in neither of our palms. Occasionally, Eliot or Marvell deserve a little gentle teasing, but we would be delighted if our efforts served as an introduction to new readers and gave them the incentive to seek out the originals. There should be as much here for neophytes as for the *cognoscenti*. Whilst we are both daily involved in the business of teaching and writing about literature, it would be equally pleasant to know that we had also encouraged re-acquaintances with poets once known, now forgotten, by former students of poetry whose paths have taken them away from the groves of Academe. And we hope that all is offered and received in a spirit of good humour. We can all agree that some of Wordsworth's poems would have been improved with better jokes (or *any* jokes). We needn't be serious about poetry all of the time.

Sometimes it is a specific poem we have tinkered with; at other times the end product is rather a composite compendium of several poems. In each case we have tried to render specific aspects of the author's style or concerns that will be familiar to readers of the originals.

It should go without saying that modern verse is easier to ape, yet it is still worth commenting upon. We have both been disappointed by our joint inability to take on some of the stalwarts of the canon, but the more we considered, the more we realised that the quality of both thought and language intertwined in a line of Keats, for example, was simply too great to imitate, on any level. And that Hopkins' sprung rhythm was, indeed, a spring too far. And that led us on to ponder who we can really call *great* amongst the moderns, in the way that we all acknowledge, say, Milton, to be great.

Without disrespect, is anything great anymore? Is our little volume of parodies also, at some level, a book about the decline of Western verse and, as Alexander Pope would insist, therefore, also about the decline of Western culture? That is a heavy thought with which to freight our light-hearted efforts, but it nevertheless lingers in the margins, between the lines and certainly between the poems. Nevertheless, we find encouragement in the way T.S. Eliot understands one's relation to one's poetic forebears.

> The predecessors should be themselves great and honoured: but their accomplishment must be such as to suggest still undeveloped resources of the language, and not such as to oppress the younger writers with the fear that everything that can be done has been done, in their language.

And so it is that Eliot's 'April is the cruellest month' fearlessly pushes beyond Chaucer's inaugural 'Whan that Aprille with his shoures soote', both lines giving rise to our own intrepidly ludicrous, 'April is the ghoulish month, breeding / Spectres on the high street'. *Great Apes* responds to Eliot's enlivening suggestion that it's never too late to develop the language and yet we fully comprehend the secondary, derivative and necessarily unoriginal nature of our labours. *Great Apes* is not cultivated to a high degree but neither is it merely a wilderness of monkeys.

Finally, we are very conscious that the underlying *leitmotif* of this text is the city of, and history of, Canterbury which is unavoidably referenced on several occasions. We do both live in the cathedral city near the St Dunstan's area but we hope this is not too exclusive for those readers who have yet to experience Canterbury. If you are acquainted with the city, we hope our allusions add background colour; if you are not, we hope they whet your appetite for a visit. Come on a pilgrimage. April is usually the best month.

Ken Moffat & James Soderholm
Canterbury, November 2015

Mrs Hamlet

Well, strictly speaking, we never actually married,
But I knew I was *the* one and only as far as he was concerned.
Sadly, my hilariously planned fake suicide—bough breaking,
brook babbling –
Backfired spectacularly on the point of fool Laertes' pointless foil,
So that the further point—of me watching him watching me
being buried –
Was lost entirely.
He was OK, but what an arse he made of himself at my funeral,
Catching me in his spindly arms,
Hugging me harder than ever
He did when I wasn't dead,
Making impossibly mythic allusions
To show that the Prince of Procrastination
Might be a King of Grief.
But was—like all brain-boxes—
A lousy lover.
Hamlet the Great Dane? Perrrrlease…

The acting mad was fun. As usual, I did it better than him:
"You must wear your rue with a difference" –
Did anyone else actually get that? –
And I've always enjoyed singing about cocks,
In private, of course.
The look on Gertrude's face was a picture, poor woman.
In the end, marrying Fortinbras was the only option to mask
My surprising resurrection.

Now I am mostly alone, of course—Norwegian hubby has
Eyes only for foreign wood and so spends his time
Gazing pale with envy upon foreign shores,
Just like old, numinous King Hamlet.
Hell, he'd rather slay a sledded Polack
Than kiss my artfully mad hair and rip the bodice of my mind
Or stay the fuck home and make supper just once.

From Our Own Correspondent

Lonely in Damascus
I trawl itinerant bars
The night sky is resplendent
With sad benighted stars.

The boys are looking pretty
With callow amber eyes
A missile makes its progress
Above the Syrian skies.

Elsewhere in the mountains
Jihadists in their caves
Measure their shallow progress
With shallow wicked graves.

"I love you God, I love you",
The mad Muezzin sings
Translated into English
"War has no ending".

Daily in the evening
I file a new report
As earth and its destruction
Is every second thought.

Outside in the desert
Silent, still and vast
A herd of feral camels
Runs fervently and fast.

A Welshman in New York

And as I was young and easy under the Big Apple boughs
Clam and Oyster full, sober and carefree handsome
Filled with the nourishing wood milk of my wordy youth
I hailed a yellow slow, mellow flowing cab
From Union aluminium shining Square
To the airy fairy Village of my whisky dreams
And the bright White Horse of my Welsh drinking years.
A Hell of a long way from Cwmdonkin Drive.

Bartender Boyo and friend of my fancy
Fix me a frisky whisky, no water in, no ice,
I get no kick from the domain of champagne
("I think that's the record!")
Clamour the amber and fiery homesick peat
Slake my snake dry, stoat sticking throat.

I was prince of the recording studios,
Famous among microphones,
More villain than villanelle yet, for all that,
Rhyming precisely in my cups, fierce tears flowing
As I prepared to join my father, there
On his sad height,
For drunk men know that dark is right
And tilt endlessly toward the mortal rub
And sing in their metrical chains
Beyond the dying light of the pub.

Angling for Saxons

Cú Chulainn, Cú Chulainn, Cú Chulainn.*

Cooling by the shores of Lough Neagh, rod
And tackle bobbing in the evening water,
The midges dancing like clúracháns,**

I heaved heavy bait into the murk-mire
Turned to my very own scop
And demanded a word-hoard, an unlocked
Phonology of Saxons, unLatinate as bloody hell
On the breathless beauty of bog-standard
English, old as hoar-frost and thicker than death.

But in my dark and bobbing meditations,
I'm suddenly back twenty, thirty years
Remembering the florid fishmonger of Toomebridge
With his grimacing barrow of hideous-looking catch,
Bloodied mouths agape and still half grinning
Like a cart of white or oily fools, part frozen,
And humming in the late afternoon breeze.

I run to the warm shelter of the baker's store
Where the sudden shadow of the bun man stuns me,
And I'm only calmed by a bottle of fresh milk
Stoppered with a newspaper talking of a war.

I'll fish no more.

Only my rod can be my pen
To pluck a plethora of phrase and fable,
A stuttered Hoo of earthy syntax and flat vowels.
A Celtic and fine angled Saxon hoard,
Torque and talk and *riastrad*,***
The sound and Hound of Ulster
To bite and tear the English word.

* Irish mythological warrior from the *Táin Bó Cúailnge*

** Clúracháns are surly, and frequently drunk, cousins of the more popular leprechauns.

*** Cú Chulainn's terrifying battle frenzy.

Leaving the library after long slow hours

Leaving the library after long slow hours
With suitable insouciance and flowers
That I may or may not present tonight
To Monica, Maeve or another flight
Of fancy. I think of the wanton girls not kissed
And imagine yet another evening pissed
On sherry, or the warm red wine I've left
On the shelf, like me, unkempt and bereft.
Maybe writing first, toss off a quick verse,
Or listen to jazz, I don't know what's worse;
Oh Hell! Oh shite! The canting night appears
And brings with all the worst of my fears
I hide from daily.

Spurn Point, Spurn Head. A spurned life badly led.
Well, that's a theory I don't always buy
Being on the edge of things can be read
As a useful way of living for the guy
Of everyday matters, the man in the street
Doesn't care much for crows or other things,
Usefully keeps his eyes upon his feet
And sees what each evening gradually brings.

Though Mine's a bicycle-clipped life I fear,
Wobbling home over Yorkshire rutted lanes,
No problem for me, some churches, some beer
Returning to a cheerless flat again.

Others jet off after women, jolly dogs,
And travel to hotter climes and all that bull,
Not for me the Belgies, the wops or frogs;
I settle for the fleshpots here in Hull.

I wake before dawn, the mist on the park.
The streets are silent in the morning freeze.
Life is first boredom, but on days like these,
I think I'll have a quick wank before work.

I Chop Vegetables While Listening to Beethoven

I am making spaghetti sauce, sipping red wine, listening
to Beethoven and, of course, thinking of Dad.
Roughly chopped vegetables would baffle, if not agitate, him.
The components must be reduced to their molecules –

diced even to protons.

Chunky sauce is an Oedipal gesture,
a rebuke to his engineered life.
And yet he lives in my hands, even as
they spare the knife and spoil the sauce.

On Penistone Crags

Striding down Top Withens one May evening,
Narrow and rocky path to Ponden Kirk,
I glance down the granite slope and see
The Fairy Cave of hopes so long believed.

Suddenly, cast back in time, a young American girl
Is laughing as she runs through the hole in the base rock.
She'll be married within the year, and so she is;
The legend never disappoints.

I look sharply upwards. A crow or chough
Hovers wisely, surveying the fading day,
Dips once, then hightails it over Middle Moor Clough.
I follow his path. The louring cloud on the moor
Makes this no evening for looking backwards
In the deep landscape of our shared mythology.

Cathy. Heathcliff. Heathcliff. Cathy.
I pull my collar tight to my chin.
Place boot firm down in rock and moss
And head for the lumb-reeking, limestone cottage
That is now and solid and shall forgive.

And I know tonight to light no candle
Lest she should breach the glass again.

The Road to Arras

I walked with one to Malvern's Gallows' Wood
One morning, late November. It was still the war
And we were glad to flee deadening words from The Front,
Talked in easy companionship of poets,
The world; world without end.
Oblivious to all but the grind of the late
Mistle thrush and crunch of boot
On well-remembered lanes.

Then, suddenly, up springs Old Bott,
Brute of a gamekeeper, like a pier head bully
Brandishing his rifle. We measure up the odds
And at once the glowering morning is incensed.
The first action a draw, but, angered still, we beat a path
And stand firm at Grove Coppice, the Old Smithy
Between Ryton and Redmarley and face down our foe.

This time Bott aims the rifle at me
And I fail. One leads me by the arm
To the welcome shelter of deep, bird-filled woods.
"Get out of here! Sling it! You posh sods!"

And, afterwards, retreating, the still grind of
The thrush jarring tightened nerves, I know,
Like an owl's hoot, a bomb will break my heart
And endlessly on the muddy, unfamiliar roads
There will be another anger, deep and grinding
And rifles and rifles before I sleep.

A Shropshire Fad

This is the trump of Doomsday
　That's heard throughout the land,
The ravaging of England
　While Ludlow Tower still stands.

We've given you a plateful
　Of rare exotic grub,
And turned your local boozer
　Into a gastropub.

For you can find ingredients
　From every county torn,
And make the chefs of Europe
　So sorry they were born.

We'll start you off with crab cakes
　That ne'er the county knew,
Garlic lamb and samphire,
　Then coffee and Shropshire blue.

Our menus are imposing
　In Becasse and Underhill's,
Our tables are impressive
　With blue remembered frills.

The High Street it is buzzing
  With rather cool wine bars,
The night sky it is blazing
  With golden Michelin stars.

This is not food from Shropshire
  Not local food at all,
But it will line our pockets
  When Ludlow Tower shall fall.

Autumn 1928

The winding stair to the light and the half-light, looking
West to The Burrah, Corco Mudruadh and The Claddagh
And the tombs of our fathers. Ireland, our Ireland.
From these battlements of The Castle of the Heroes
I have surveyed all, and by all been surveyed,
Asking question of everything and all,
Ascending, ascending in the visionary gyres
Then flailing a line to the dark waters below
So earth and light and sky and Heavens can meet.

A poet should live in a Tower;
The midnight candle glimmering
As a beacon on the lonely road to truth
For the late, lost traveller, out of sight,
Urged on by celestial nightingales
While truculent peacocks sulk by night.

But, another damp Autumn has broken me.
Despondent, I must disperse once more,
Too filled with passionate intensity
Than ever this poor frame was before.
And I bequeath with most solemn vow
This stark tower and laborious stair,
In the certain knowledge that it must now
To another soul pass, or to disrepair.

I turn away and shut the door.
Forgetting and forgot, a long day is done
The time for departure is almost nigh,
A few precious memories to gather then I
Shall impossibly sail toward Byzantium.

X

Opening another late birthday card,
That marks a day I no longer celebrate,
I squinny without my glasses quite hard
To read the necessary verses, lightweight,

And then the scrawling, near legible hand
Wishing me well in a tight, cursive text,
From another far corner of this dead land
And I note that it finishes XXX.

How sincere are lines of Xs like this?
How warmly meant and how much do they say?
Do they mean the warm embrace of a kiss?
Or are just a dead cipher we use every day?

I think about the Xs in all our lives,
We fritter them about like desperate fools,
The Xs that we send to friends and wives,
Or the Xs on my father's football pools.

They denote a draw. A futile dead end.
Like a long, goalless deadlock between the sexes.
Check mate, full time or journey's sorry end;
A few of my wives have descended to exes.

X men, X files or piercing X-ray eyes,
X, can't write my name but still want to vote,
An X across a name means it is excised
Xmas: just another word for bloat.

X marks the spot on all good treasure maps
And X is across on mathematician's graphs,
And X is just wrong in upper or lower caps
A final reminder of all our sorry gaffes.

And talking of crosses I suppose that we
Can't forget the X that came from Golgotha
The mythical crucifix, or just plain tree,
Those planks of wood that caused all the bother.

And so, as I place it on my mantel sill,
I have to come to terms with something hard
Though the day to me may mean nothing still,
Those Xs just meant nothing on my birthday card.

The Merchant's Prologue

A Marchant was ther of a noble Suisse banke
And for his richesse al men him thonke
And al men heeld him in high parage
Yet but he was eight and twenty yeer of age.
Yrekened he with diligiaunce in his ipadde
Al his chevissaunce, whether good or badde.
Wel koude he in eschaunge sheeldes twisten
And specially when thilke sheeldes nat existen.
Ful faire and fetishly were clasped his bootes
And ful wel biloved was he atte Coutts.
To liven in delit was evere his wone
He was Epicurus' owene lovede sone.
Dronke hadde he in al his time
Manie a draughte of sweete reede wyn.
Thogh the bacon was nat for him at Dunmowe,
For wyfhood was to him a state unknowe,
He was a worthy man in al degree
And yeve he freely unto charitee
Of oothere manly men in fressh Vauxhalle
He yaf nat a pulled hen for thinges smale.
Quentin men him callen after that good Seinte,
But close freendes mooste him clepen just Queynte.

a tic

k

l

in

g

there

it

gr   o   w

s

flesh rising   to

care s   s

i lostmyse

l f

in her pour

in

g

in her wet

larg   ess   e

we d

a

nc

ed

all

n ight

in that

c   afe

near the

ed   ge

of the

uni

v e r   s

e

An Horatian Ode upon Blair's Return
from The Middle East

Insanely men themselves declare
Their enmity for Tony Blair,
    Shadow cabinet sings
    Glory everlasting.
From Fettes College fetters freed
He forged anew the Labour creed,
    Bored by gowns at St. John's
    New Labour myrmidons
Emerged to bring the unions down
And put the red flag back in town;
    Did thorough their own side
    Their fiery way divide.
He felt the hand of history
And holidayed in Tuscany,
    But through advent'rous wars
    Urged his active star.
They say he faked a dossier
That helped to take us all to war,
    Found not a smoking gun;
    Was the fault of Mandelson.
Forget not his Balkan glory
Or the Northern Ireland story –
    Blair's first ever present:
    Good Friday Agreement.
And if he faked Iraqi plots
Was just to plant the Bergamot,
    What other fitting tree
    For innocent Cherie?

Retirement never planned or sought
From his rightful place at court,
   Traitors their debts have paid,
   Brown thoughts in a Brown shade.
And now the Middle East resounds
To our Hero's tender sounds
   Ninety nine grand per speech
   In hall or on the beach,
So let the common people's prayer
For Anthony Charles Lynton Blair
   High round the houses sing
   Ours, theirs, the World's King.

The Pound Land

For TSE
La prima scimmia

As I manoeuvred to get alongside, I was asking myself, 'What does this fellow look like?' Suddenly I got it. He looked like a harlequin. His clothes had been made of some stuff that was brown holland probably, but it was covered with patches all over, with bright patches, blue, red, and yellow—patches on the back, patches on the front, patches on elbows, on knees; coloured binding around his jacket, scarlet edging at the bottom of his trousers; and the sunshine made him look extremely gay and wonderfully neat withal, because you could see how beautifully all this patching had been done.

Conrad.

April is the ghoulish month, breeding
Spectres on the high street, mixing
Milkshakes and desire, feeding
Tourism sweets to keep its ghosts alive.
Winter kept them skiing at Chamonix
Or some other place of slopes and dosh
Where the urchins bank their holy days
Before the spring breaks the spell of snow
And sends them on the pilgrimage
To scratch down notes on Thomas Becket –
"That's where they cut his stupid head off" –
And there's Henry on shuffling knees –
A bit of rhythmical humbling –
Before the devouring of souvenirs.

Defective Christian beauty
Post Samothrace—to kalon
Market place.

I watch them from my coffee shop
As they turn left on Mercery Lane,
Measuring out their banalities
With coffee spoons as they come and go,
Their sacred quest turns questionnaire
On their Norman Invasion, *Part Deux.*

Iz theez Bootz?
No, c'est Pret À Manger. See the French words?
Giggles and then, *But where iz Bootz?*
Straight down there, cent metres
À droit.
Saint Boots à Canterbury –
Good for what heals you.

M'sieur?
Ou est Le Gap?
Quest que c'est Le Poundland?
C'est maintenant et en Angleterre, n'est ce pas?

Thousands upon thousands every week
Flow past the Palace and up Sun Street
To murder a Cathedral.
I had hoped death would undo some of them.

I stay awake most of the night
And am hung again most every morning.

    Why don't we do it in the road?
    Why don't we do it in the road?
      No one.

Fallout on roses and radioactive kittens

    No one will be watching why don't –
    The road. Okay.

There's the Wife of Bath (Bath is dead)
The lady of situation comedies,
The heterotextual riding forth
To bag husband number whatever.
Childless, she, forever.
When she's good she's very good
But when she's bad she's better.
Mind the gap-
Toothed Wife
Who once was.

Gather ye. Rosebud. Xanadu.
Woollen mittens, warm.
Ragged claws, scuttling.
Gentile or Jew? Achoo! Achoo!

Ring a ring a ring a ring
At five o clock –
Mourning.

We live as we dream—alone.
Not even journeys of the heart can save us
From the intense inane
Of ash-heaps and millionaires.
The nymphets have departed –
Fire sermon of my loins –

This menacing verse I have set loose
In the doggerel eat doggerel world.
Dr T.J. Eckleburg sees all, a bespectacled Tiresias.
Hypocrite fabbro, mon ape, mon frère.

The clouds broke over Canterbury
And the pilgrims disgorged themselves
Into the car park near Sainsbury's.
This island. Such footprints. Bad Fridays.

The tastelessness of the tired town –
Becket's dead
Marlowe's dead
Josef Teodor Korzeniowski's dead –
What shall we put on their eyes?
        A pound.

The bland leading the bland, ceaselessly,
To the park, park, park –
They all go into the park
And plant their hyacinths around
The burial mounds of the dead.

And there's the fat Monk on his high horse –
Is it perfume from a dress that makes him
So transgress?

Post-real Margate,
The harbour JWM turned to account,
His swirling pallet raising tempests
Like a Prospero of paint.

Now cracked mud, detritus, lost ugly things
Find homes in the Contemporary
Where the local girl made good,
Spreading her scratched legs to give birth
To the formulated shock of weary
Pilgrims who ventured there hoping
To see at least one canvas from the old master
Only to find a dirty stick on a stained mattress
(Even Duchamp would flush to see it)
Under gleaming fluorescence that makes
All good light hide in the sundering sleeve.

Emin Emin
Eminem Eminem
Duff duff duff duff
O that Shakespehearean rap
It's so inelegant
It's so
        Crap.

In the poet's shelter the helpless
Stare out to sea, roll cigarettes and mumble
Their lives into shape for half an hour.
Heaps of broken promises –
Toiling to let sad souls drag
Rat bellies along the slime
Of the nothing new.
The cricket gives no relief
No, nor the rugby either.

London, Jerusalem, Dumpton Park.
Too real.
Guinness Guinness everywhere
Nor any drop for us.
Only a shelter with no soul
Shape without substance
Mockeries without talent
Poiesis frisking itself
Encountering no resistance.

O Lord save me but not yet *ferchrissakes*.
Let force bewitch you.

Of human bondage from East Kent
Over to morns in Somerset
The unkindness of strangers in the night
On whom we rely to tram
Our desiccating desires –
To do, to be,
To be, to do,
The prepositional phrase loses steam
In the cooling twilight of our chaos.
O tempora! O mores!
World world world
And that's an end on it, without end,
To the last syllable of recorded
Please   Time   Hurry
Furious sound, signifying signifiers.

Shall I at least set my blandness to rights?
Fish and chipping with the strip mall behind me.
Death by lager: what the liver said.
Mad England hurt me into parody.

O o o o that Lady Gaga's persona –
She's so cocky
But not in a co co rococo way.
Too puffed.

De gustibus non est disputandum.
Longtemps, je me suis couché de bonne heure.
Where they have burned books
They will end in burning human beings.
The final stroke of the Ninth—a phenomenon.
There is nothing either good or bad
But thinking makes.
　　Young bride, bridegroom
　　　CONTRA NATURAM
Freunde! Seht!
Fühlt und seht ihr's nicht?
So priketh hem Nature in hir corages,
Cruel, sudden,
Purpled nail, blood of innocence.
Images heaped, raving sluts, tilled.
Thou ravished bride, unquiet.
Sedition and the tumorous talent.
Fieri sentio et excrucior.
Rivets, what I really wanted was rivets.
These dilapidations I have whored into ruins.

On Margate sands, I conflate nothings
And Crusoe myself with some regret,
A patient log man looking for brave Miranda
To lean into the dark matter –
'Tis new to thee –
Of an increasingly expensive multiverse.
Wild geese when, the moon –
The windows failed, then, I could not.
Arrest. The silence.

Dadaism Dumbledore Didi
Let's hang ourselves immediately!
It'll give us...

      ...See?

          Shan
        h   t y
        a
      i n r i
        t
        i
      S h a n t y

The Charge of the Night Brigade

*The Crimea was becoming a popular venue for stag nights
before the present troubles began.*

Half a beer, half a beer
Half a beer onwards
All in the alley of death
   Fell the sick kindred.
"Charge for the bar!" he said
Into the alley of death
   Fell the sick kindred.

Wine bar to left of them,
Wine bar to right of them,
Wine bar behind them
   Trolleyed and chundered;
Showing their satin thongs,
Voices aloud and long,
Alcohol jaws of death,
Lager and Jäger Bombs,
From their mouths vicious songs
   Sang the sick kindred.

Flashed all their arses bare,
Showed off their pubic hair,
Scaring the locals there,
Puking their bitter bile
   All the world wondered;
Submerged in heavy smoke
No foreign words they spoke,
   Beer and Black Russians;

Theirs not to make reply
Theirs not reason why
Theirs but to drink and die,
    Into the alley of death
    Fell the sick kindred.

Oh what a night they had!
"Blimey mate, we were mad!"
    All the world wondered.
Yalta to Volgograd
The Night Brigade they were bad
    Wretched sick kindred.

I Never Saw a Blackamoor

I never saw a blackamoor,
I never saw the wine-dark seas,
Yet I know how lilacs look,
And how cold stone must please –
I never spoke with Emerson,
Nor visited his sturdy soul;
Yet Mind is my bosom-mate,
And fancy a locked door.
*
This North and South I cannot stand
The peaceful North
The bitter South –
My father has a silent mouth –
A frugal man I always ware –
I cannot cross the Delaware
Eternity, it is my land –
*
Amherst bells I never loved –
I think they ring to bring me peace
I think I wish them all to cease –
Glad that I was never loved.
*
That hope has feathers
Is all I know
Through feathered poems I do cope –
Through poems, feathers, dreams
My scope –
My poems die with me, I hope.

February Amongst the Cantiaci

Why this is hell, nor am I out of it.
Marlowe

Once and last. Spring is coming
And sun shines sharp and dazzlingly low on
Stones by which once more I stand
Here in a medieval street.
Here is History, once and now,
Violence, forgiveness, worship, ruin,
I know these things, but also know that
Everything that can be, has been seen
And done, here and now and before in this place,
Framing us all in the stark perspective
Of years of human perplexity.

Suddenly, back in a city I know,
Un-villaged amongst the Cantiaci,
A pointless pilgrim with a new routine:
Conscious of uncoupling by the railway yard,
A brave half new world of things to be seen.
A local market every morning, then
The road running down to bustling St Dunstan's,
The butcher, the baker and the amiable vintner,
Specialised shops and ancient inns,
Through one last gate and amazingly there
The whole great city unfolding before me
Familiar faces; familiar to me.

A river dissects it, ancient and slow,
And parts the languorous gardens where
Centuries of students have lain in the sun

Cleverly ignoring the work to be done.
Tourists and boatmen casually blend
In this Sylvan scene by the café of friends.

A cosmopolitan crowd, at their best,
Imperious Caesar found them cultured
Amongst all of Britannia, I find my way
Confused by newness, surprised by sightings
Of those I know, those I don't,
A known and unknown, solitary person
Leaving black prints in a February street
In a holy city where memories are kept
And ghosts rise always to startle anew.

The Cantiaci, a cultivated folk.
I like their theatre, I like their sport,
I appear at their frequent dinner parties
Like Banquo's endlessly manifest ghost;
My friends are doctors, priests, professors
A long way from what I was brought up to be,
The strange and familiar in equal part.
In return, I teach their kids,
Putting on an antique, Socratic show,
No piss-pot on my head, Xanthippe,
Though something of marital discord I know.

Past restaurants, cafés and tourist shops
The perished churches and the pillaged pubs,
Bookshops and buskers and heritage sites
Hotels and wine bars that set up, then close.
For so many years this has been my abode.

The whole town gathers to a glorious head
At the site of a vast and needy church;
From every angle it demands to be seen,
Will not be drowned out, like pain or an ache,
Old stones where despair and revenge have been
It draws us towards it and counts the hours
And gives benediction beneath its towers.
I measure out my life with ringing bells.
Harry dins the faithful to Evensong,
Shall I have faith? Shall I be full?
The tin bell of Dunstan calls the curfew.
All shall be well. All has to be well.
Spring, with no choice, is coming.

But, awkwardly nested in the thriving city
I live out days in an alien house,
Feeling, unfeeling, dazed and perplexed
And in the sullen cinema of my head
In a cushioned seat, watch the picture unfold,
An image on an endless burning loop,
The camera zooming cruelly in,
On two hands parting, silently,
Rings flashing madly in the brutal sun,
As fingertips part and one, or both,
Fall into the inferno, once and last,
And finally as the plangent violins swell
And I climb the stairs for a helpless night
I know I'm damned to a Faustian Hell
And there to dwell on what we've lost,
And what we did and what it cost.

Kitty Hodge

They sculpted Kitty Hodge, to stand
Unruffled, lost in time;
His likeness is just off the Strand
Far from the madding crime
Of that gentleman of England
Who killed cats in their prime.

Young Hodge the kitty never knew –
Safe in his Georgian home –
The meaning of the man who flew
To shoot the cats that dared to roam,
Or why a casement was his mew
Secure upon a tome.

Now little portion of Gough Square
Will Hodge for ever be;
The sable fur and wistful stare,
His base, the Dictionary;
As much an avatar as heir
To Johnson's legacy.

Yomp

We shoot—shoot—shoot—shoot—fighting in Afghanistan!
"Keep—your—eyes—peeled!"—huntin' Terry Taliban—
(Yomp—yomp—yomp—yomp—yompin' up and down again!)
   There's no honour in this war!

Road map—shock and awe—fightin' for the oil fields,—
Troop surge—Middle East—sendin' in the Navy Seals,—
(Yomp—yomp—yomp—yomp—yompin' up and down again!)
   There's no honour in this war!

Route march—Desert Storm—Help for Heroes—understand—
Truck stop—IED—losing comrades in 'Elmand.
(Yomp—yomp—yomp—yomp—yompin' up and down again!)
   There's no honour in this war!

"Right! Left!"—Arab Spring—regime change in Libya,
Three—four—thousand bombs—dronin' down on Syria,
(Yomp—yomp—yomp—yomp—yompin' up and down again!)
   There's no honour in this war!

Why—should—we—care where the bad insurgents go?
"Hands up!"—water board—Lock 'em in Guantanamo.
(Yomp—yomp—yomp—yomp—yompin' up and down again!)
   There's no honour in this war!

In a Station of the Tube

The melancholy of these faces on the staircase,
Pansies on the Way Out.

Good Morrow

I wonder, by my troth, what thou and I
    Did while we loved? Were we not pleased, even then?
You sucked on country pleasures certainly
    And maybe I slept in Bacchus' warm den?
'Twas so, but then all pleasures fancies be.
If ever any pleasure I did get
Which I desired or not, 'twas but despite thee.

And so good morrow to our parting souls,
    Which watch not each other at all I fear;
But rather stare from two disparate poles,
    Both frozen, both bleak, neither kind nor near.
Let new astronauts to old planets go,
Let polar explorers strike out in snow;
They shall never find a place that you and I shall know.

When two stiff twin compasses broken be
    There never can be answer or theorem new,
What questions we had be now futility;
    I no longer you, you no longer me.
Whatever dies was not mixed equally;
Seven parts you and only three of me –
Thus, love doth turn to dust, desperately.

Not Saying but Thinking

Nobody noticed her, the clever woman,
But she noticed everything;
I kept it all inside me –
Not saying but thinking.

She had Mrs Dallowayed herself
Into a bundle of sensations, a thousand-eyed
Creature who kept silent about the endless
Tediousness and toil of human beings.

All people, except dead people, are a pain
In the arse, she observed to herself.
And they were perfect pains in the arse just before
The grave quietened them down for good.

The world was always too much with her
And now she's half-mad from politeness –
Not saying but thinking.

The True North Road

Driving home from Poly, end of second term,
not hitching this time, I'd borrowed an old car
from a posh college mate with more cash than sense,
provisional licence in the back of my jeans.

The True North Road, cassettes in the dash,
baccy for the journey and fuel in the tank.
The long straight road that takes us all home
to Amarillo, or Yorkshire Route 66.

The knockabout comedy of the Alconburys:
are they in? The Stukeleys? Are they at home?
Little Gidding to the left. If I came this way
taking the route I'd be likely to take,

or came at night like a broken king
it would be this way, The Great North Road,
and my end would be in my beginning
and my beginning still in my sorry end.

"You Great Ponton!", I hear my father say
as we laugh and decide to abandon Turpin
in Stamford, just past the Ram Jam Inn
which always sounds rockier than it really is.

Through a disappointed Sherwood Forest,
that never makes me quiver, "All for one, one for all!",
or was that the other lot? I forget. It's late.
Tired and bored, I pull up for a piss

at Rocco Forte's Pleasure Palace at Woodall,
am randomly tempted to torch the forecourt

for the hell of it. But I don't, just this once
and, instead, spark up by a crap Little Chef.

Here the air is colder, the language thicker,
like we've tapped to the root of the native tongue,
my vowels are starting to flatten, like tyres.
Now, this is Ermine Street, the Saxon Road,

to Scotland or Scotch Corner or, at the least,
as far from Portsmouth as it's possible to come.
"Drive careful, love" says the girl selling gum.
The air is sweeter, sharper, truer.

Did I leave home for knowledge or just to stand
on my own two feet? Or for Geography?
'Environmental Systems' firm in my head
for the first year exams that await my return.

Either way, it's a long, long drive and I wonder
once again why I moved so far from all
the once familiar things coming back to me,
environmental systems that make me burn.

Turning west now away from the great artery
of England to the country's stone backbone,
Carboniferous limestone and millstone grit,
moors to the left of me, Bradfield, Midhope,

two terms of college firmly behind me,
wiser, more foolish than when I first left
I dip the headlights as a car leaves a farm;
Denby Dale, Holmfirth, Slaithwaite, Marsden.
Home.

Limp, Mortal Muse!

Some men bubble over pansies and thorns
As if nature dresses for the occasion
To supply the bard with plenteous horns
For his sublime and fruitful inspiration –
But my Muse delights in what it mourns
And bruises every expectation –
As if it feasted on rancid meat
Or learnt to frolic with misshapen feet.

I called Wordsworth "Turdsworth" just for a laugh –
He took it badly, the pietistic tool,
Who thought his verse kernel to the chaff
Of my rebellion against his poetic gruel.
I found my mad muse in a large carafe
And soused the poet's daffodil school.
I was "poaching on his manor", he claimed,
Plagiarising pansies—was I thus defamed.

Coleridge dabbled in the flighty abstruse,
His metaphysics drove us all insane –
Forcing his capacious mind like a goose,
Until his tortured soul was all but slain,
In his warring Mind he never called truce –
For the tragic Coleridge: no pain, no gain.
His Mariner is a genius of loss,
His Muse, an unlucky albatross.

John Keats gave onanism a bad name –
Images to him were courted lovers
Over which he brooded until from they came
Voluptuously between the covers

Of books that would bring the lad no other fame
Than to be used as nesting for plovers –
For in drowned Shelley's pocket did we find
Evidence of Keats's saturated mind.

Speaking of Shelley, that Promethean spark –
Never could I fathom his boundless glee:
His schlepping of light into the dark,
His encomia on Humanity,
His radical beliefs, wide of the mark,
His misguided Defence of Poetry.
All that prattle about birds that never wert
And mountains so vast they make your head hurt.

My mortal Muse always kept me in check –
It's hard to be lofty when you're an imp.
When I staggered to Greece, the Turks to wreck,
All of existence seemed to me to limp –
No doubt cynicism hobbled my trek:
The world was either a whore or a pimp.
So, in London I had not a single mourner
And they kept me well out of Poets' Corner.

Autumn Diurnal

Many animals, especially apes, are diurnal.
The American Heritage Science Dictionary

The barica he sat in like a burnished throne
Glided through the scum, the poop was beaten black
And black the oily water of the foetid canal,
Past chocolate factory and the BSA,
The Mitchells and Butlers' Tudor-fronted pubs,
The sad river captains watched on in silence,
Dumb Enobarbs helpless to stem the steady,
Incessant progress of the sable, sleek boat.
And on he went from Gas Street black Basin
Past Charon's crossing, an obol for each trip,
Manically singing Homer in a Dudley accent,
The strings as false as an African queen,
Descending the last long, inevitable flight,
Onwards, onwards and all the time wondering

Why did he marry Fulvia and not love her?

To a Spouse

Robert Burns was a countryman and most of his liaisons were with like-minded country lassies who were only too familiar with the birds and the bees.
George Scott Wilkie (2004)

Wee spindle, gentle, honest thane
You have but your ain self to blame
If I've broke up your lovely hame
   Like a sleekit rat.
I am not proud, I'm only sayin',
   A man's a man for a' that.

I'm truly sorry our communion
Has broken up your marital union,
Her red, red lips have been her ruinin'
   O' foggage green.
If it's o' help to ease your musing,
   We were nae seen.

'Twas but a tryst in heather shady
With a married, sonsie, maidie
But my nine inch did please your lady
   Nidge, nodge and leeze her.
I may have left her with a baby
   I guess and fear.

Her groaning gyvel I did fill,
Her hurdies like the Grampian hills
Among them all I had my will,
   Daub hard and drivin'.
And heard her roaring' loud and shrill
   At my double divin'.

But fellow, thou art no thy-lane
In thinking that your love's in vain,
The best laid wives of trusting men
    Gang aft agley,
Whether tae leave us grief and pain,
    Ah cannae say.

Wee birkie, c'ad a lord, who cares?
If Scotland is to win, she shares,
All men shall taste the bill of fare,
    It's right, ye ken.
And I have had the ploughman's share
    And am the king of men.

Whinge!

for Thomas Becket

I

I saw the mediocre minds of my generation further corrupted
    by political correctness, fatted pious swaddled in scaly jargon,
    swanning themselves along boulevards at twilight looking
    for a really fresh sushi fix, coiffed academics publishing their
    perished souls as monographs on writers rightly forgotten,
who were welcomed in the academies for cultural studies and
    disability studies and queer readings of straight texts,
who played it safe and wrote confessional drivel and abstract
    nonsense and passed it off as lyric poetry,
who clawed at whores in Amsterdam but never once caressed
    the great stone where
    Rembrandt crushed his lapis,
who created a world of deconstructive teeth with nothing at last
    to chew on but the bitter cud of well-mulched mendacities,
who studied Joyce and Beckett only to 'go into' advertising and
    make us buy shit we don't want to impress people we don't like
who ate Prozac and medicated and medicalised pathologised
    lobotomised themselves into a stupor of niceless and
    vomitous fairweather nihilism
who went on with vapid thoughts to lead vapid empty States to
    casual desolation
    feng shui-ing through their luxury non-smoking apartments
    with shit blonde furniture
    and bio yoghurt and the priceless coffers fell to the bankers
who spent the load on Krug or Mumm at a thousand bars across
    the foetid city
    licking cocaine from the breasts of the establishment
who fed the inglorious multitudes an endless diet of Soma crap
    big brothering them out of existence or locking them up in
    101 Hell.

II

What threadneedle creature of cement and aluminium bashed
  open their skulls
  and imagination?
Mammon! Filth! Ugliness!
  Ye cannot serve poetry and Mammon. Traders sobbing on
  Wall Street! Bondsmen chained to their desks! Martha
  Stewart with a glue-gun and a pinecone!
Mammon, whose coffers brim with glib priests! Mammon who
  treasures dirt! Mammon who treasures death!
Mammon, whose buildings are cost-effective. Mammon, who
  feeds jihadists who feeds capitalists, who feeds itself with the
  fury of a jet-engine pissing itself off!
Mammon, whose world is a closed system of tears! Mammon
  astride a grave and a difficult birth! Mammon, who banks
  souls without interest.
Daymare of Mammon! Mammon the bloated breast! Mammon
  the shrivelled dug! Mammon the cliché! Mammon the
  platitude! Mammon the palaver! Mammon the jejune!
Mammon the insipid! Mammon the flatulent! Mammon the
  banal! Mammon the mind-forged manacle! Mammon the
  sodomite of Art!
Mammon, whose hand clutches fear in handfuls of broken
  images!
Mammon in whom I loaf at ease and do nothing over and over!
Mammon in whom I sip my cozy life and mark essays and build
  the pension! Mammon the rapist of intuition! Mammon the
  hoover of puissance! Mammon the cashiered Talent!

48

III

Thomas Becket! I'm with you in Canterbury
   where your three quarter head sleeps just down the street
I'm with you in Canterbury
   where the Norman bad boys took you down.
I'm with you in Canterbury
   where you are deader than I am
I'm with you in Canterbury
   where you anointed the feet of the poor and addled the king.
I'm with you in Canterbury
   where they murdered you three times, Fitzurse, Cromwell
   and Eliot
I'm with you in Canterbury
   in the name of Jesus and for the protection of the church
I'm with you in Canterbury
   where we out-sermon each other from the Archbishop's
   pulpit
I'm with you in Canterbury
   under the red light of the martyr's lamp in the Crypt
I'm with you in Canterbury
   where a thousand mad churchmen sing the *Nunc Dimittis*
   forever
I'm with you in Canterbury
   where Bell Harry measures out our lives in thankless
   repetition
I'm with you in Canterbury
   where demented market traders still sell your precious
   image for peanuts

I'm with you in Canterbury
   where faithless pilgrims wander on ghost legs to find your
   shrine,
   famished tourists who like you as a martyr but love you
   as a pub
I'm with you in Canterbury
   where we lay down our lives for our beliefs, endlessly,
   despite the
   mad rantings of oilmen and bankers,
   and parliamentarians and the pointless parochial posh
I'm with you in Canterbury
   in my nightmare you walk to the North West Transept to
   lose your pious head
   over and over with increasingly blank recognition
I'm with you in Canterbury
   in my dreams you walk brain dripping and holy from
   your dark Martyrdom,
   through the brutal and cheap streets in tears, sodden and
   uncomprehending,
   to the door of my turbulent house in the Canterbury
   night.

Mummy

I bit him because of you.
You pushed me, you pushed me,
Push me, pull you,
Red shoe.

I was a genius at two.
By one, I got off the floor,
By two I could jimmy the door,
But a heart cold, ice-wise New England wind blew through.

Your hand me down, ball gown, college education,
From Cambridge to Boston to Cambridge, oh you!
At first was a gas till I busted my ass
For Panzer men, first one, then two.

You saw me marry number two,
A hawk to my mushroom,
Cold as any ancient trout –
And so blue, so blue.
Ach du!

From womb to tomb,
Jarred in-between, I flew,
All because you spread your soul
To let a bad man fuck you –
Fuck you.

Mummy, mummy, you bitch! I'm you!

Lines on Omaha Beach nine days before the 70th Anniversary of D-Day

There was no intuiting that morning
In a grain of sand, the bad
To worse to death of 2499 men
Caught between Germans
And the surge of the tidal
Atlantic pushing the leaking dead
Into their shocked bodies as they realized
Someone had blundered.

My hands mechanically sought blood-red
Stones from the beach to take home
To two soldiers in the family, proving
I had been there, done my American duty
To honor the horror.

Dead to the dead, I perform the perfunctory
Sea-stroll and reflect commonplace reflections,
Squeezing the stones in my pocket
To get blood out of them.
But there was no imagining the morning
Of those men pushed into the streaming lead
Of history.

In the cemetery above
Omaha, I complete the ritual,
Pulling my camera up to salute
Rows of ghosts, all standing at attention –
Posing.

Spears of Self

1

I ejaculate myself, and fling myself,
And what I celebrate you shall celebrate
For we are all atoms and Adams frolicking
In the great American garden of Anthem.

I repose and I toss my soul,
I repose and touchingly observe a spear
Of my exuberant and excitable selves –
I am largesse. I contain new platitudes.

Conventions and traditions are corpses to me.
They held me in check, damned me up good for a time.
Now I am body electrical, circuits gone wild.
An immense world of unencumbered delight
Inflamed by my senses five.

2

A few light kisses on the disporting breeze
Blow to my newfoundland, a more than Aoelian music to charge
The atmosphere with the tingling love of the stroking hand.
Every last bit of me is soiled with rich fertility.
Every tongue in my savage soul outreaches Orpheus.
Every metaphor seizes and spills and brims with salubrious panic.
I am mad to let the oak trees rub up against me.
I am mad for the flaming green grass to comb through tingling nerves.
My armpits stench the horizons, heavy musk more subtle than steam.
There is no part of squirrels that is not part of me.
The very moon dances in my limbs, pulls me into torrent.

3

Over the Northern soldiers I hover like a lover.
Over their steaming wounds I warm my hands.
I kiss their dying life from their simple young mouths
And hold their delicate souls in my mouth, like butterflies.
I ruffle the fur on the chests of dead men,
I watch them trundled to the great heaps,
And celebrate their manly, mortal heroism.

4

You shall find your own way, mentor-less.
You shall not be disciple to creed or crux.
You shall follow the single commandment of self,
Abjuring all else that does not thrill to your touch.
You shall shape your own spheres and spears
And exult in the sacrament of the moment,
In the tremulous Zephyr whose sweet breath
Caresses you into fountains of longing and self-praise.

Is my cheerfulness obnoxious? Is my heart a trumpet section?
Is my soul an allegro without end,
An andante of thrilling tenderness?
Very well then. There is no happy sound that is not me.
Owls, foghorns, train whistles, shrill cries in the still night.
I am every sound that blows through the belching city.
I am every twittering skylark scudding airy heights.
My heart is an echo-chamber for every thing that lives.
My mind is a tuning fork for the symphony of the wide world.
An aching chorus of long delight effuses from me and for me.
Songs of innocence and experience stroke each other.
The body comes apart, pleasure without origin or end.
For mine is the kingdom, the power and the glory,
Forever and forever, to the last syllable of tempestuous time.

5

The balding eagle races down to see who is howling
So ecstatically and loafing so wonderfully.
I too am a swooping eagle, I too am uninterpretable,
I string my barbaric harp over the roofs of the world.

The final bits of dusk await me.
I am coaxed into a dew and infinitely patient star-dust.
I take my leave as heir to no man, nor woman either.
I diffuse my flesh in whirlpools, and float it in frothing bubbles.

I give myself to the ashes, to the stars, to the green spears I cherish.
If you need me you can find me under your fingernails.

You can't have a clue what the hell I am thundering on about.
But I will nevertheless be fruit and fibre to your works and days.

Failing to fathom me do not abandon all hope,
If you can't find me in locomotives or armpits or crotches of oaks,
You must never give up looking for me.
I recline in the suppleness of words waiting for you.

The Midland Grand Hotel

Thank heavens for sense and a sense of the past
The St Pancras Station is going to last,
That single span gothic held up with firm ribs
Can still be seen proudly from church caryatids.

A short walk from Euston they've put up a pub
That's serving warm beer and ridiculous grub,
We can't all be choosers in this rescue game
They've had the bald cheek to have stolen my name.

Oh such a delight to restore them so well,
Those great dreaming spires of The Midland Hotel,
Victorian splendour and neo-gothic
Oriel windows and red Gripper brick.

Inside in the booking hall there is a bar
For wetting your whistle for the restaurant car,
The music is ghastly and cocktails too sweet
And the girls from Poland are run off their feet.

For screwdrivers, gin slings or a whisky sour
A pleasant enough place to surrender an hour,
Watching the travellers with cases on wheels
Heading to Europe for fabulous deals.

I see there's a statue of me like a berk,
Commuters will pass it on their way to work.
A hand on my hat and my brolly aside
I look like a vicar who's mislaid the bride.

The trains they still journey to Hove and Flitwick
The carriages are clean and the engines are quick
The people upon them seem shallow and mean,
There's a shabby old crowd on the seven fifteen.

But still, mustn't grumble, my work is complete,
We've rescued this gem for the man in the street,
For those who still know what is right and is not
There's cake, there's bubbles for Sir Gilbert Scott.

Sonnet 155

When I do count the clock that tells the time,
Eternal numbers to out-live long date,
With means more blessed than my barren rhyme,
As subject to time's love or to time's hate;
When I consider everything that grows
Growing a bath and helpful remedy
To give full growth to that which still doth grow;
To that sweet thief which sourly robs from me.
How can I then return in happy plight?
I am to wait, though waiting so be Hell.
Upon thy side against myself I'll fight,
From this vile world, with vilest worms to dwell.
　　Yet do thy worst, old Time, despite thy wrong,
　　Tired with all these, from these would I be gone.

Lines
Written a few feet above
St. Augustine's Abbey
on revisiting Canterbury during
a Pilgrimage
13 July 2014

Ten years have passed, with the length of ten grim
Winters, and once again do I behold
This oak tree reaching with its aching limbs,
As if to crave alms of the young sun,
Its pale leaves folded and wrinkled
Like the withered hands of some ancient
Beggar stumbling through the frozen night
To make his rude nest under winking stars.
But *these* tiny leaves unfold to new life
And spread their open hands to the sky.
Quercus alba!—oldest and dearest Friend!
How oft, in moments of deepest distress,
How oft have I turned to thee, mighty oak?
The clover at my feet another tale
Repeats of the passing of old time,
Decay, despair, the weakening heart
And all that ten years can heave upon
The pensive, fraught and beleaguered soul
To teach it how to suffer the wisdom
Of an unintelligible sadness,
How we see into the death of things.

But how oft, amid the howling city,
Pent up in the prison-house of others,
How oft have I turned to thee, thou
Spreading oak, the many-flowered fields,

The surging Stour after heavy rains –
How oft have I turned to the blessings
Of Nature to repair my heavy heart
And mend the frayed and tattered soul?

And yet
Even if I could not nurse my being
With the loveliness of trees and rivers
Would I the more despair, for deeper thoughts
Impress and move the subtler mind –
Thoughts that dwell in the mystery of all
That stirs in the mighty heart of Nature
And pace in piety through the abbey
Of the self-delighting soul of man.

Nor, perchance,
Had the cloister of my own mind served not
To protect and nurture my blasted heart
Should I fall into a Slough of Despond.
For thou art with me; thou, my Brother Bard!
And in the mimicry of your talents
I can always hear the tuneful echo
Of a fellow pilgrim lost like myself
In the dark wood of our middle ages,
On our journey into the fresh torment
Of our mad, mendacious modernity.
Nor will we ever forget that we two
Mocked our moment into tolerable shapes,
Re-versing each other harmoniously,
Like simple blacksmiths, our forge, our abbey,
The bounteous Goods Shed spread around us,
A large beaker of wine our evening meal
When there we met to break bread with the dead.

Life Sentences

You're fading and disappearing this Autumn
Like a Sanctus sung as a choir boy sings,
Self-accused and faithless and yet, to us, a wit,
Of useless reference and the hardest learnt things.
A deep remembrance of things past;
I hope the maple flourishes at your last.

Your bored, capricious stage persona
You would have us thought just a shallow guise,
But was more like the sturdy tarot fool;
Only through ignorance can we be wise.
The truth, I suspect, is further away;
For a sad man, sorrier than he could say.

Part clown, part gravedigger, more than that,
A fatter, balder Hamlet talking Strine,
Conducting to your entire dissatisfaction
Your fallible self, your febrile, foolish mind.
The rest may be silence, it always is,
The dumbfound shock of death's cold kiss.

A brilliant, keen and curious observer
You seemed to us to have all that life gives,
Learning, humour and a language as sharp
As a paper cut, that stings, but lets you live.
Something well said remains day after day,
Is something we can not ever wish away.

Warnings to the young and well are savoured
Dwelt on, relished, but do not last,
Larking like children in Auden's wood
We soon return to the present trash.
Oblivious to what the world really shows,
The days we live are just days we know.

Quickly our minds return to trivia,
Not loved ones, but things we didn't do
Or have, not the maple turning colour
Or birds or bees or fish or dew;
Lost in a strange, superficial glow,
We reap what we unconsciously sow.

I read your *Observer* reviews in the bath
I thought it fitting, time and again,
You presented as a great Australian Ape,
But beneath that was a fine Cambridge brain,
But a brain, however brilliant, bleeds,
The warnings you sent us we will not heed.

Your final late flowering verse was stunning,
Shocked like brilliant autumn blooms,
Moved us, but only will return
When our own sad height finally looms
Over where our destiny endlessly leads,
We read, but do not believe what we read.

And now at the midpoint of my life
You serve as a frightening *memento mori*,
Not the entertainment I once craved.
Your poems have hardened into glory:
The Australian punter is home from the hill,
Whether or not we like it, we've had our fill.

Memoirs of the dying become yet more poignant
However unreliable you think what they say,
The book of your enemy is still remaindered,
But your sentence of death remains day by long day.
For whom the bell tolls, it is tolling still.
For whom should a sky so full stay still?

I hope the maple flourishes at your last
For a sad man sorrier than he could say.
The dumbfound shock of death's cold kiss
Is something we can not ever wish away.
The days we live are just days we know,
We reap what we unconsciously sow.
The warnings you sent us, we will not heed,
We read, but do not believe what we read.
Whether or not we like it, we've had our fill.
For whom and for why should a sky so full stay still?

Legends of the Apes

Mrs Hamlet

This poem is how it all began. The day after Carol Ann Duffy had given a brilliant recital at The Langton, we began to knock around an idea about Ophelia faking her own suicide (echoes of *Romeo and Juliet*, obviously) in order to test Hamlet. After throwing back and forth fragments by e-mail, the conceit began to develop into the disastrous denouément of marriage to the Norwegian wooden-topped Fortinbras. We wished to stay faithful to the Poet Laureate's sardonic tone in her own delightfully irreverent *The World's Wife*.

From Our Own Correspondent

The notion of Auden as a war reporter seems to fit with Orwell's description of him as "A Boy Scout communist", certainly not as a front line fighter. Of all the 'thirties poets, he is the one most difficult to imagine joining the International Brigade or imitating John Cornford or even Orwell himself. He attracted great criticism for disappearing to America for most of the duration of World War II. We grant it is hard to imagine him in Syria. His travel companion, Louis MacNeice, in their *Letters from Iceland*, pleasantly observed, "Everything he touches turns to cigarettes".

A Welshman in New York

Apart from the doffing of the cap to Sting in the title, this composite Dylan Thomas focuses on his legendary or apocryphal final drinking session in The White Horse Tavern in Greenwich Village, where the self-styled 'Rimbaud of Cwmdonkin Drive' claimed to have downed a record eighteen straight whiskies before staggering off to die. The Village can do that to a man. We remain implacable in our belief that the recording studio was nearby. And that eighteen straight whiskies is no excuse to go home and die.

Angling for Saxons
Although a figure from Ulster legend, it seemed right to align Seamus Heaney with Cú Chulainn whose *riastrad*, or war frenzy, wreaked havoc on his enemies (and sometimes on his own side). If we believe Roman Jakobson that literature is essentially, 'organised violence done on everyday speech', Heaney, more than anyone, can be seen to be one of the most violent writers of the Twentieth Century. And we unLatinated as much as we could. A clúrachán is a type of leprechaun that goes out to drink after the daily chores are completed. We know that feeling.

Leaving the Library after long slow hours
Alas, poor Larkin. Had his letters not survived his death, English Departments in universities across the land would have viewed him, unanimously, as a genius, rather than making the cardinal error of conflating man and poet and diminishing the latter because of the former. We are led to believe that his collection of pornography was almost unrivalled in Europe (and certainly unrivalled in Hull). However, if Larkin could write the unforgivable 'Love Again', he could certainly have written this poem. Poor Maeve.

I Chop Vegetables While Listening to Beethoven
It is possible to ape unconsciously. That this slight Billy Collins riff appeared just as a midweek supper was being prepared is testament to his lasting credibility as an urban poet talking to other urban dwellers about little tragedies

between the ears. Collins has bucked the trend and proven that you can make money from poetry. His move from The University of Pittsburgh Press to Random House secured him a six figure fee for a three-book deal. Keep at it, kids.

On Penistone Crags

Ponden Kirk is a gritstone outcrag north of Top Withens and just a few miles from Haworth, West Yorkshire. Local legend dictates that any woman passing through the hole at the base of the rock will be married within the year. It is both delicious and impossible not to imagine Hughes and Plath walking there and always impossible not to see them as Heathcliff and Cathy. (c.f. Plath's 'Wuthering Heights') Surely Plath would have dared pass through the rock hole? The impact of the highly recommended *Birthday Letters* is clearly evident in this poem. A colleague has observed that there is no way choughs would occur on Middle Moor Clough. This is not only picky, but disallows the faint possibility that Hughes was simply having an off day as an ornithologist. More vitally, there is no other native bird we know of that rhymes with 'Clough'.

The Road to Arras

Is inspired by Matthew Hollis' superb biography, *Now All Roads Lead to France*, and his hypothesis that Edward Thomas' decision to enlist might have been due to his self-perceived failure of nerve during an encounter with a gamekeeper while out walking with his friend Robert Frost. It was not possible to resist invoking Frost in the poem's last line. Thomas died unusually; a bomb blast nearby stopped his heart whilst he was serving at the front near Arras in 1917. He had previously been considered extremely lucky for two very narrow escapes involving various bits of ordnance. Who knows what gems he would have gone on to write? For what it's worth, we hold fast to our description of a mistle thrush as sounding as if it's grinding machinery. Whatever you think.

A Shropshire Fad

Inspired both by AEH and the fact that Ludlow was nominated the food capital of England in 2013, a fact we are sure would have bewildered him, as indeed would the menus. We are pretty sure Housman was more a pie and a pint sort of a lad. No disrespect meant whatsoever to the establishments of Becasse or Underhill. We would be delighted to hear forthwith if the Housman burger has been invented in Ludlow.

Autumn 1928

Yeats' beloved tower, Thoor Ballylee, was impossible to inhabit in the winter months owing to rising damp and he abandoned it entirely in 1928. Given the loving references to the Thoor in both *The Tower* and *The Winding Stair*, it is hard not to imagine what a wrench this would have been for the poet, further so given the proximity to Lady Gregory's home. We are prepared to hear disagreement but, in our experience, peacocks are, generally, truculent creatures. In many ways, we feel that William Butler Yeats was always overshadowed by his artist brother, Jack, who won a silver medal at the 1924 Paris Olympic Games for his painting 'The Liffey Swim'.

X

Tony Harrison's V is so visceral, powerful and intriguing that we couldn't help but imagine how someone so generally unsentimental in his writing would react to the everyday schmaltz of a birthday greeting card with its vacuous x-marked kisses. One X begat another until our poem emerged. In many ways *V* is still the most powerful poem of the 1980's and the Channel 4 broadcast of Harrison reading it in the churchyard where his parents lie buried is still a must watch.

The Merchant's Prologue

Is of course entirely re-written. Chaucer's Merchant has a cynical view of marriage so it was both easy and a delight to reinvent him as someone keener on his own sex and, as a nod to the current *zeitgeist*, a despised modern banker. We would be lying if we said that we had no specific, personal merchant banker in mind in this depiction. We do, however, apologise for the anachronism of Vauxhall, a Seventeenth Century pleasure grove that Chaucer could not have envisioned. Well, not without taxing it till its pips squeaked.

42

E E Cummings made the world safe for fridge-magnet poems, which is something of a blessing, well-disguised. For who has not delighted in concocting slightly-agitated midnight word-salads on someone else's ice-box, highball in hand, giggling at one's own ludic lyrics capering to life? Of course, Cummings was an artist, not a prankster, but his work is still altogether apable. Cummings is the one who so wisely observed that "America makes prodigious mistakes, America has colossal faults, but one thing cannot be denied: America is always on the move. She may be going to Hell, of course, but at least she isn't standing still". Indeed, she is not. She is nothing if not auto/mobile.

An Horatian Ode upon Blair's Return from The Middle East
Whilst a great poet, Marvell did write some tosh, none
more so than his 'Horatian Ode on Cromwell' which both
time and history have shown to be embarrassing, naive
and sycophantic. Not to mention cruel. This is revenge for
having to teach the poem to generations of blank-faced Sixth
Formers who just do not get it, and neither should they. The
fact that another political leader often crudely described as a
war criminal was in the news in the Middle East around the
time we were writing this was just fortuitous happenstance.
We have always warmed to Marvell's stated practice of never
drinking more than two cups of wine in another man's house,
but happily wading into the second bottle in his own home.
You just can't be too careful.

The Pound Land
The Waste Land cries out for parody more than any other
poem of the Twentieth Century. Without detracting from
the poem's status as the inaugural voice of High Modernism,
this was too much fun not to do. We just did the police in
different voices. And we still think Virginia Woolf was too
prissy for deriding Eliot as repressed, reserved and buttoned
up "in his four piece suit".

Charge of the Night Brigade
Let us all agree that Tennyson wrote much better poems
than 'The Charge of the Light Brigade'. We have also written
better parodies, but we still blame the former for the latter.
Famously prompted by *The Times* newspaper, Tennyson
allegedly sang the poem aloud on the chalk ridge near his
home on the Isle of Wight before returning to his study and

committing it to paper. We're glad we weren't out walking that day. If you've heard the wax recording of him reciting it, you would be too.

I Never Saw a Blackamoor

As we discover with Larkin, privacy comes at a premium for poets. The fact that the Amherst Belle didn't really intend to publish her own poetry was no disincentive to her sister to publish reams of the stuff after her sibling's untimely death. We were intrigued by the story of the visit of the great Ralph Waldo Emerson to Amherst and the agonies Dickinson went through not to meet him, despite her worship of him. On a less portentous note, Emerson also visited Driffield, East Yorkshire, the home of one of the authors, to deliver a lecture to The Mechanics' Institute. One really has to ask, why?

Spears of Self

Walt Whitman's tumultuously-ebullient style in 'Song of Myself' was waiting to be imitated, with what justice our gentle reader can determine. We have heard Whitman described as obnoxiously-optimistic, but then in 1850 America had not fallen into such howling disrepair.

Kitty Hodge

The occasion of this poem was happening upon the statue of Hodge in the courtyard outside Dr Johnson's House in Gough Square, London. Thomas Hardy's elegiac 'Drummer Hodge' sprang to mind just as one recalls the anecdote about Johnson's deep affection for his cat and fear for its safety with a cat-killing maniac loose in London.

Yomp
Kipling was a keen parodist himself and produced *The Muse Among the Motors*, a kind of early *Great Apes*, but on the theme of the motor car. Here our parody shows a slightly darker vision of war than the simplistic view of Empire and its enemies evoked in *Barrack Room Ballads*. Re-reading these now, it is easy to see why Kipling has fallen from fashion. If you have a hankering to seriously terrify your children, play them Kipling's own reading of 'Boots'. It really does show that some poets should not be seduced into recording their own poetry.

In a Station of the Tube
Ezra Pound's imagist poem is justly famous for its presenting 'an intellectual and emotional complex in an instant of time'. We remind the reader that the word 'pansy' comes from the French 'pensée'— 'thought, remembrance'.

Good Morrow
No poet writes better love poetry than Donne and if your wish is to find that elusive creature, 'wit', there is perhaps no better poet to start with. Witness his epitaph on the disastrous effect of his secret marriage on his blossoming career: "John Donne, Anne Donne, Undone". Donne's *Songs and Sonnets* are required reading as is John Carey's superb study, *John Donne: Life, Mind and Art*.

Whinge!
Ginsberg's 'Howl' has, in our judgment, enjoyed undue reverence. His poem nearly apes itself and so it was no trouble to update its shrieking conceits and echo its famous

'cadence'. Ginsberg himself was aping the godfather of the Beat generation, Walt Whitman, but turned affirmation into rant and jeremiad.

Mummy

Perhaps the least subtle and most obvious of the apes. It is based on the bizarre revelation that on the first night Plath met Ted Hughes, at a party in Cambridge, she bit him, quite hard, on the cheek. We think this should have given him a clue as to what he was in for. Plath's grave at Heptonstall is enormously moving by the simple fact of being so understated. However, we wonder how she feels bearing the name to eternity of Sylvia Plath Hughes.

Not Saying but Thinking

Stevie Smith's 'Not waving but drowning' comes into focus here, but at an angle. In this case the speaker's polite restraint keeps anyone from reading her signals.

The True North Road

Of course it is ridiculous to imagine that Simon Armitage would travel up the A1 on his way back from Portsmouth, reading Geography, to the West Riding, but perhaps he stopped off *en route* for some reason and travelled east? Either way, the A1, or Great North Road, is a familiar and comforting path for all Northerners returning home. And the ancient route certainly has ancient roots. If Simon Armitage did take this road, I'm sure he would be as amused by the place names as we have always been. Dry Doddington, Long Benton, Great Ponton…That the Ram Jam Inn is now closed should be a cause for national

mourning. We do apologise for presuming upon a living
poet and re-imagining a personal life.

Limp, Mortal Muse!
Byron was so adept at *ottava rima* in his comic masterpiece,
Don Juan, that we could only hold a tiny candle to his
ingenious use of that Italian verse form. Amongst all the
Muses of Afflatus in the Romantic Period, Byron's alone had
a sense of humour and a satiric stinger in its formidable tail. It
is pleasant to imagine that Byron's frisky, light-footed poetry
happily compensated for his having to drag his clubbed foot
around the world until his swampy death in Missolonghi in
1824. It took the poetic establishment, and the government,
until 1969 to give him a little plaque in Poets' Corner.

Autumn Diurnal
Poet and classicist Louis MacNeice settled at the University
of Birmingham where he wrote the brilliant *Autumn
Journal*, hence the hideous pun in the title, and Birmingham,
Shakespeare and Virgil are all referenced in this short poem.
Whether or not Birmingham has more miles of canals
than Venice is a question still not settled to our satisfaction,
though it is still a mystery why local boy, Shakespeare, has not
a hint of a canal in either of his Venetian plays. Later, in 1948,
whilst working for BBC Radio, MacNeice wrote to his wife
while she was away to inform her, "Dylan T. stayed the night
at 52 & yesterday we gave up to recreation:—Lords in the
morning, wine bar at lunch time, Oval (where I'd never been)
in the afternoon & London Casino in the evening". Now
that's a day out we would have loved to have joined. And we
doubt there was very much cricket actually witnessed.

To a Spouse

'I pray draw near and lend an ear/And welcome in a Frater,/
For I've lately been in quarantine,/A proven fornicator'.
(Burns, 'Ye jovial boys who love the joys'). Rabbie Burns was
called to account by the Kirk Session for fornication. He
also had twelve children by four different women, including
nine by his long suffering wife, Jean Armour, who herself
admitted "Rab should hae twa wives". If you think this verse
is bawdy, have a look at 'Nine Inch Will Please a Lady'. Burns
long nurtured an interest in erotic verse and songs but, even
more fascinatingly, became the first person ever to feature on
a commemorative bottle of Coca Cola in 2009. Equally oddly,
The Black Bull Inn in Moffat, Dumfries and Galloway, used
to have a window pane upon which Burns had inscribed a
short poem, but the window was bought and transported to
St. Petersburg in Russia, of all places.

The Midland Grand Hotel

Was, indeed, inspired by an afternoon drinking too many
cocktails at the splendidly restored baroque Gilbert Scott
bar at St Pancras Station. It is easy to mock Betjeman as
an old establishment fuddy-duddy, but his support, along
with Sir Nicholas Pevsner, for the survival of this glorious
building in the face of calls for demolition, means, in
practical terms, he achieved so much more for the nation
than a clutch of the great poets put together. Though we
rather like it, I suspect he would have found fault with the
statue in his honour at the station.

Sonnet 155

Come on, work this *cento* out.

74

Lines Written a few feet above St Augustine's Abbey
From the abbey of his mind, the remarkably unremarkable
Wordsworth produced so much distinguished and self-
regarding blank verse that finally he realised how much
he had been talking about himself, and kept his great
autobiographical poem, *The Prelude*, in a drawer until the
great man was pushing up daffodils, rolled round in earth's
diurnal course with rocks and stones and trees. 'Tintern
Abbey' (as his poem of 1798 is customarily known) is that
epic in small and we have attempted to ape its style and its
idiom whilst updating the meditation for our time and place.
It crossed our minds that Wordsworth and Coleridge went
for peripatetic wanders and collaborated to bring out *Lyrical
Ballads*, an inaugural text of British Romanticism.

Life Sentences
Clive James is one of the most underestimated cultural
observers, poets and critics of his generation, but nowhere
is his skill better demonstrated than in his poignant final
collection *Sentenced to Life*. We make no apologies for
using occasional lines from James' own work in this poem,
celebrating both his work as a writer but, also, his disarming
self-deprecation, turning to bitter self-recrimination at the end.